MADE YOU LAUGH!
JOKES FOR KIDS

Other books by Sandy Silverthorne

Crack Yourself Up Jokes for Kids
More Crack Yourself Up Jokes for Kids

MADE YOU LAUGH!
JOKES FOR KIDS

SANDY SILVERTHORNE

SPIRE

© 2020 by Sandy Silverthorne

Published by Revell
a division of Baker Publishing Group
PO Box 6287, Grand Rapids, MI 49516-6287
www.revellbooks.com

Printed in the United States of America

Library of Congress Cataloging-in-Publication Data
Names: Silverthorne, Sandy, 1951– author.
Title: Made you laugh! : jokes for kids / Sandy Silverthorne.
Description: Grand Rapids, Michigan : Revell, a division of Baker Publishing
    Group, 2020. | Audience: Ages 6–12
Identifiers: LCCN 2019046545 | ISBN 9780800737665
Subjects: LCSH: Wit and humor, Juvenile.
Classification: LCC PN6166 .S5685 2020 | DDC 818/.60208—dc23
LC record available at https://lccn.loc.gov/2019046545

The author is represented by WordServe Literary Group www.wordserveliterary
.com.

22   23   24   25   26   7   6   5   4

To Vicki and Christy: You guys are the best.
You make life so fun. Thanks for all your help on this
book and for letting me try out lots of jokes on you.
And for laughing in all the right places.

To Stan Beard: You taught me how
to have fun loving God. Thanks.

What goes *dot-dot, dash-dash, squeak-squeak*? A message in Mouse code. Ha! Made you laugh! Want to hear a joke about paper? Never mind, it's tearable. Made you laugh again! Whether you have a quiet little giggle or a side-splitting guffaw, this book is guaranteed to make you laugh. And if it doesn't, you need to have your funny bone examined.

What do you get when you cross a chicken with a robber? A peck-pocket.

This book is filled with hilarious stories, one-liners, riddles, knock-knock jokes, and lots of crazy, silly illustrations. It also has some totally tough tongue twisters to test your tongue-twisting talents. So what are you waiting for? Go for it! Go ahead and make your friends, your brothers and sisters, your teacher, and even your parents laugh! And while you're at it, make yourself laugh too!

Q: Where do cows go to have fun?

A: To the amoooosement park.

Q: What kind of bee can't make up its mind?

A: A maybee.

Patient: Doctor! I'm convinced I'm a pumpkin. Can you help me?

Psychiatrist: Sure, I think I can carve out some time in my schedule.

Patient: I keep dreaming I'm in a washing machine.

Doctor: Wow! What happens?

Patient: I toss and turn all night.

Q: What has lots of ears but can't hear?

A: A cornfield.

Knock, knock.
Who's there?

Ammonia.
Ammonia who?

Ammonia little kid. What do you expect?

I'm an exchange student.

Q: What do you call a droid who always takes the long way?

A: R2Detour.

Q: How do you make a lemon drop?

A: Just let it fall.

Q: What do you call a duck who gets straight A's?

A: A wise quacker.

$E=Mc2$

Q: How do you talk to a giant?
A: Use big words.

Q: What do you call two birds who are in love?
A: Tweethearts.

Q: How does a scientist keep his breath sweet?
A: With experi-mints.

Sunday School Teacher: Why is it important to be
                quiet in church?
      Kid: Because people are sleeping?

Teacher: Nick, who invented fractions?
Nick: Henry the 1/8th?

Rowan: I went riding this afternoon.
Remy: Horseback?
Rowan: He sure is. He got back about an hour
before I did.

Q: Where does Pharaoh go for his back pain?
A: To the Cairo-practor.

Reporter: How did you like that new restaurant on Mars?

Astronaut: The food was great, but there wasn't much atmosphere.

Q: What did the astronaut say when he crashed into the moon?

A: "I Apollo-gize."

Ron: How do pickles enjoy the weekend?

Jon: They relish it.

Bill: What do you call an old snowman?

Phil: Water.

Tongue Twisters

Tie twine to three tree twigs.

She should shun the shining sun.

Fred threw thirty-three free throws.

Skunks sat on a stump, and the stump stunk.

Mix, miss, mix.

Q: What do you get when you cross a centipede with a parrot?

A: A walkie-talkie.

Ben: How do novels stay warm?
Len: They put on their book jackets.

Aiden: Did you see that cop dressed as a pilot?
Caden: Yeah, I guess he's a plane-clothes officer.

As soon as you find out someone has ten thousand bees, marry them. That's when you know they're a keeper.

Tourist: What's the fastest way to get downtown?
Local: Are you walking or driving?
Tourist: Driving.
Local: That's the fastest way.

When someone tells me to stop acting like a flamingo, that's when I put my foot down.

Knock, knock.
Who's there?
Yule log.
Yule log who?
Yule log the door after I come in, won't you?

If a gang of robbers all jumped into a pool at once, would that be called a crime wave?

CANNONBALL!!!!

Al: I told my boss that three companies were after me and I needed a raise.

Sal: What companies?

Al: Gas, water, and electric.

My uncle used to be a banker, but then he lost interest.

Q: What goes *ha, ha, ha, plop*?

A: Someone laughing their head off.

Q: What did the beaver say to the tree?

A: "It's been nice gnawing you."

Q: What's the difference between your elbow and a rabbit's cell phone?

A: One's a funny bone, and the other's a bunny's phone.

Jenny: How do porcupines play leapfrog?
Benny: Very carefully.

Q: What do you get when you cross a porcupine with a balloon?

A: POP!

Bill: How do chickens dance?
Jill: Chick to chick.

Hannah: What goes *dot-dot, dash-dash, squeak-squeak*?

Anna: A message in Mouse code.

Dot-dot dash-dash
squeak-squeak

Q: What do you call a pan flying through space?

A: An Unidentified Frying Object.

Iris: Why did the astronaut bring scissors, paper, string, and glue on his trip?

Bo: He wanted to do spacecrafts.

Q: What's an astronaut's favorite beverage?

A: Gravi-tea.

Q: How do you make a baby go to sleep in space?

A: You rocket.

Q: What's a cow's favorite party game?

A: Mooo-sical chairs.

It was a terrible summer for Humpty Dumpty, but he had a great fall.

Len: What did the bankrupt cat say?
Ben: "I'm paw."

Mike: Which nail does a carpenter hate to hit?
Ike: His thumbnail.

Joe: Why was the archaeologist upset?
Bo: Because his career was in ruins.

Ron: How many magicians does it take to change a light bulb?

Don: Only one, but he changes it into a rabbit.

PRESTO!

Q: Where do geologists like to spend their time?

A: At rock festivals.

Terry: Why did the bank teller stand right next to the vault?

Jerry: He wanted to be on the safe side.

Joe: My dad gets paid for making faces.
Flo: Wow! Where does he work?
Joe: In a clock factory.

Ed: Why don't hot dogs act in the movies?
Ned: The rolls are never good enough.

Q: What's a tree's favorite drink?
A: Root beer.

Chloe: What's tall, French, and delicious?
Kylie: The Trifle Tower.

Q: What did the scissors say to the hair?

A: "It won't be long now."

Q: What's a frog's favorite year?

A: Leap year.

Q: What's green, hops, and can be heard for miles?

A: A froghorn.

Knock, knock.
Who's there?
House.
House who?
House it going?

Knock, knock.
Who's there?

Alaska.
Alaska who?

Alaska only once. Open the door!

Knock, knock.
Who's there?

Wooden shoe.
Wooden shoe who?

Wooden shoe like to know?

Mason: Why did Sammy run past his classroom?
Jason: He wanted to pass his test.

Randy: Why did the teacher wear sunglasses in her classroom?

Andy: Because all of her students were so bright.

Camper: How do you know that's a dogwood tree?

Ranger: I can tell by its bark.

Q: What illness can a plane catch?

A: The flew.

Ron: What was the spider doing on the computer?

Don: Designing a website.

Peg: What do you get when you cross detergent with a composer?

Meg: A soap opera.

A guy went to a home improvement store.

"Yeah, I'd like to buy some boards," he said.

"How long would you like them?" the worker asked.

"Oh," he said, "a long time. I'm building a house."

Knock, knock.
Who's there?

A door.
A door who?

Adorable me—that's who!

Knock, knock.
Who's there?

Oscar.
Oscar who?

Oscar if she can come out and play.

Knock, knock.
Who's there?

Henrietta.
Henrietta who?

Henrietta whole pizza by himself.

Want to hear a joke about paper? Never mind, it's tearable.

Q: How does a penguin build his house?

A: Igloos it together.

Teacher: Christy, please spell *wrong*.
Christy: R-O-N-G.
Teacher: That's wrong.
Christy: Isn't that what you wanted?

Teacher: Jenny, can you tell me where the English Channel is?

Jenny: I can't. We don't have cable.

Ben: Why couldn't the bicycle stand up by itself?

Len: It was two-tired.

I wouldn't buy anything made with Velcro. It's a total rip-off.

Asher: I've come up with a groundbreaking invention!

Bo: What do you call it?

Asher: A shovel.

5/4 of people admit they're bad with fractions.

Jenny: I'm thinking of going on an all-almond diet.

Benny: That's just nuts!

Knock, knock.
Who's there?
Annie.
Annie who?
Annie body home?

Knock, knock.
Who's there?
Al.
Al who?
Al give you a kiss if you open this door.

Q: What spends all its time on the floor but never gets dirty?

A: Your shadow.

Q: What animal needs to wear a wig?

A: A bald eagle.

Q: Where do fish keep their money?

A: In the riverbank.

Len: I'm taking up rock collecting.
Ben: How's it going?
Len: I'm picking it up as I go along.

Jill: Why did the kids bring honey to the teacher?

Will: Because they were all bee students.

Q: What do you call a flower that runs on electricity?

A: A power plant.

Q: Why did the dog get all A's in class?

A: Because he was the teacher's pet.

Q: What do you call a shoe made out of a banana?

A: A slipper.

Iris: What's a skeleton's favorite musical instrument?

Harper: A trombone.

Q: How do billboards talk to one another?

A: Sign language.

Peg: Did you hear about the bedbug that was expecting?

Meg: Yeah, she's going to have her baby in the spring.

Q: How did the farmer meet his wife?

A: He tractor down.

Q: How do astronauts keep clean?

A: They take meteor showers.

Ava: Why are you taking your computer to the shoe store?

Fred: It needs to be rebooted.

Chad: Why did the café hire the pig?

Rad: He was really good at bacon.

Give me a shingle with a shimmy and a shake!

Q: What did the hot dog say when he crossed the finish line?

A: "Hooray! I'm a wiener!"

Jill: What kind of car does Mickey Mouse's girlfriend drive?

Phil: A Minnie van.

Q: What's a little bear's favorite dessert?

A: Cub cakes.

Rowan: Why shouldn't you tell a joke while you're standing on ice?

Ava: Because it might crack up.

Jim: What did the barber say to the bee?

Tim: "Do you want a buzz cut?"

Jeremiah: Last night I dreamed I was a car muffler.

Brooks: Wow! What happened?

Jeremiah: I woke up exhausted.

People are usually shocked when they find out I'm not a very good electrician.

Peg: Where do you learn how to make banana splits?

Meg: At Sundae school.

Rancher: Where do cows buy their clothes?

Farmer: From cattle-logs.

Oooh. That's a cute moo-moo.

If you take your watch to get fixed, don't pay the guy before; wait till the time is right.

Q: What do you call a snake wearing a hard hat?

A: A boa constructor.

My friend borrowed my grandfather clock. Now he owes me big time.

Chloe: My mom turned thirty-two yesterday
and had a really short party.
Kylie: Why?
Chloe: It was her thirty-second birthday.

Not only is this new thesaurus terrible, it's also terrible.

Ed: The ducks keep trying to bite my dog.
Ned: Why?
Ed: He's a pure bread.

Q: What did one firefly say to the other?
A: "You glow, girl!"

Q: Where do chickens like to eat?

A: At a rooster-raunt.

Q: What does a girl spider wear when she gets married?

A: A webbing dress.

Q: I have lots of keys, but I can't open any door.
    What am I?

A: A piano.

Thanks for explaining the word *many* for me. It means a lot.

Jay: What did the penny say to his penny friends?

Ray: "We make a lot of cents!"

Q: Why did the spider buy a new car?

A: 'Cause he wanted to take it out for a spin.

Q: What do you call a potato wearing glasses?

A: A spec-tater.

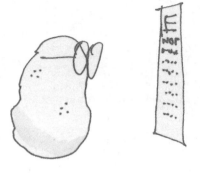

Christy: Why does a grape make a great mom?
Misty: Why?
Christy: Because she loves raisin' children.

Lonny: What do you get when you cross a parrot with a gorilla?
Donny: I don't know, but whatever he says, you'd better listen.

Ed: What do you get when you cross a flower with Lassie?

Ned: A collie-flower.

Q: What do you get when you cross a sprinter with a dog?

A: A 100-yard dachshund.

Q: Why don't banks allow kangaroos to open accounts?

A: Their checks always bounce.

Two kids were looking at the night sky.
Connor: "Wow! Is that Venus or Neptune?"
Deagan: "I don't know. I'm not from around here."

Q: Where do sheep go after high school?

A: To the ewe-niversity.

Q: What did the duck say to the class clown?

A: "You quack me up!"

Q: What's a pig's favorite ballet?

A: *Swine Lake.*

Jill: Did you hear the story about the peacock?

Phil: No, but I heard it was a beautiful tale.

Q: What do you get when you cross a reptile with a duck?

A: A quack-o-dile.

I entered the suntan Olympics, but I only got bronze.

City Guy: Is chicken soup good for your health?
Farmer: Not if you're the chicken.

Q: What do you get if a hen lays an egg on the top of a hill?

A: Egg rolls.

Oops.

Teacher: I want to discuss your son's appearance.
Parent: What about it?
Teacher: He hasn't made one in this classroom since September.

Isabel: Why do you have that rubber band around your head?
Charlotte: I'm trying to make snap decisions.

Jill: What are you reading?
Phil: I don't know.
Jill: But you were reading out loud.
Phil: I know, but I wasn't listening.

Diner: I'll have the steak, and make it lean.
Waiter: Yes, sir. To the right or the left?

Tongue Twisters

Tragedy, strategy.

Cinnamon, aluminum, linoleum.

A slimy snake slithered through the sandy Sahara.

So this is the sushi chef.

How can a clam cram in a clean clam can?

Teacher: Jimmy, do you need a pencil?
Jimmy: Yeah. I ain't got one.
Teacher: Jimmy, where's your grammar?
Jimmy: She's at home, but she ain't got no pencil
either.

Doctor: Can you breathe in and out for me three times?

Patient: Are you checking my lungs?

Doctor: No, I need to clean my glasses.

Teacher: Why did Robin Hood only rob from the rich?

Kid: 'Cause the poor didn't have any money.

Q: Where do hamsters go on vacation?

A: Hamsterdam.

Asher: What do you call it when five hundred stamps escape from the post office and run down the street?

Harper: A stampede!

Q: What can you hold in your right hand but not in your left hand?

A: Your left elbow.

Q: What fish performs operations at the fish clinic?

A: The sturgeon.

Hello, I'm Dr. Bass. I'll be your sturgeon.

Woman: Doctor, I keep getting smaller!

Doctor: Well, I guess you'll have to be a little patient.

I gave all my dead batteries away today. Free of charge.

Jim: I'm going to become a candlemaker. It's so easy.

Tim: What do you mean?

Jim: They only work on wick ends.

I broke my finger last week. On the other hand, I'm okay.

Q: Where do pigs go when they're sick?

A: To the hogs-pital.

Max: Why can't sheep drive a car?

Alsea: 'Cause they can only make ewe-turns.

Q: What's a dog's favorite snack?

A: Mutt-zerella cheese.

Terry: I bought a drum for my cat.

Jerry: Why's that?

Terry: She's a purr-cussionist.

Joe: How do you keep a rattlesnake from striking?

Moe: Pay him a decent wage.

Phil: Why aren't koala bears considered real bears?

Bill: They don't meet the koala-fications.

Never criticize anyone till you've walked a mile in their shoes. That way, when you do criticize them, you're a mile away and you have their shoes.

I'm terrified of elevators, so I'm taking steps to avoid them.

Q: What do snowmen eat for breakfast?

A: Frosted Flakes.

An older couple was driving through Wenatchee, Washington, on a vacation. They kept arguing about how to pronounce the name of the town. When they stopped at a fast-food place, the man went to the counter and asked if the worker would pronounce where they were, real slowly. The worker responded by saying, "Buuuurrrrgeerrr Kiiiinngggggg."

Every time I see an autobiography on the bookshelf, I just skip to the "About the Author" section to save time.

Dan: I just got some pills from the doctor for my sleeping problem.

Jan: So why do you look so unhappy?

Dan: You have to take one every thirty minutes!

Q: Why can't the Three Bears get into their house?

A: 'Cause Goldilocks the door.

Q: What's a lawyer's favorite food?

A: Sue-shi.

Q: What do you get when you cross a small bear with a French dog?

A: Winnie the Poodle.

Mom: Why do you make so much noise when you eat your cereal?

Kid: Teacher said we should always start our day with a sound breakfast.

I went shopping on an empty stomach yesterday. Now I'm the happy owner of Aisle 7.

At my last job interview, the manager said he was looking for someone responsible. I told him that whenever anything went wrong at my last job, they always said I was responsible.

Adam and Eve were talking one afternoon in the Garden of Eden.

      Eve: Do you really love me, Adam?

   Adam: Who else?

    Terry: Where do fish sleep?

    Jerry: In the riverbed.

I got in trouble yesterday at customs. They said, "Papers?" And I said "Scissors!"

Mom: Aiden, did you do your chores?
Aiden: Yes, mom, I just polished off a chocolate bar.

Dentist: You need a crown.
Patient: Finally, someone who understands me.

Q: How do you make a hot dog stand?

A: Take away its chair.

Q: What does a snail say when he's riding on a turtle's back?

A: "Wheeee!"

Mom: Where's your report card, Sam?

Sam: I loaned it to Jaxon.

Mom: Why?

Sam: So he could scare his parents.

Just kidding.

Sal: Why did the watchmaker go to the doctor?

Hal: He was all wound up.

Q: What's worse than a giraffe with a sore throat?

A: A centipede with athlete's foot.

Rick: My kid is afraid of Santa Claus.

Nick: Oh, Claustrophobic, huh?

Kylie: Have you ever seen a fishbowl?

Iris: No, but I've seen a cowhide.

Terry: What's a soccer player's favorite color?
Jerry: Solid gooooaaaaalllllld!

Always buy a thermometer during the winter. Because during the summer they go up.

Teacher: How many feet in a yard?
   Kid: It depends on how many people are standing in it.

← FEET

Fred: Who was on the phone?

Remy: I don't know. They said it's long distance from Hong Kong. I said, "It sure is," and hung up.

Teacher: Lucas, please use the word *fascinate* in a sentence.

Lucas: My jacket has ten buttons, but I can only fascinate.

Teacher: Who can tell me what a *myth* is?

Connor: A female moth?

Q: What do elves do after school?

A: Their gnome-work.

Teacher: Who leads all the orcas?
Deagan: The Prince of Wales?

Come on, everyone! Follow me!

Hannah: If we breathe oxygen during the day, what do we breathe at night?
Chloe: Nitrogen?

Sal: What's the hardest thing about falling out of bed?
Al: The floor.

Alsea: Why do you have an egg in your bed?

Caden: 'Cause I want to get up at the crack of dawn.

Q: Why was the wisdom tooth all dressed up?

A: Because the dentist was taking her out that night.

My brother borrowed my bike. I told him to treat it as if it were his own. So he sold it.

Dan: What do you get when you cross a tiger with a lamb?

Jan: A striped sweater.

Q: What did the astronaut say in a press conference?

A: "No comet."

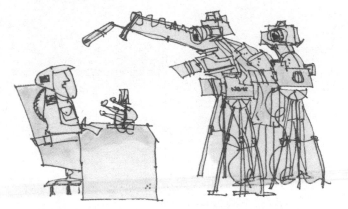

Knock, knock.
Who's there?
Champ.
Champ who?
Champoo the dog. He's really muddy.

Q: How did the explorer discover the glacier?

A: He had good ice sight.

Did you hear about the auto mechanic who was ready to re-tire?

Let's hit the road.

Swimmer: Hey, every time I go scuba diving, I hear music.

Lifeguard: Oh, it must be a coral group.

Patient: Are you the head doctor?

Jim: No, I'm the foot doctor.

Q: What do you call a one-hundred-year-old ant?

A: An antique.

Q: Why was the centipede late for school?

A: He was playing "This Little Piggy" with his brother.

Q: How did the beetle find out all the caterpillar's secrets?

A: He bugged his phone.

Kate: What do you call an ant who's good with numbers?

Nate: An accountant.

Q: What did one light bulb say to the other?

A: "Let's go out tonight."

Q: What do you get when you cross peanut butter with a quilt?

A: A bread spread.

Q: Where does a shrimp do his shopping?

A: At a prawn shop.

Q: When is a boat not a boat?

A: When it's afloat.

    Isabel: Why couldn't the bee go to the dance?
Charlotte: 'Cause it was a mothball.

Hit the road. You don't bee-long here!

Chad: Where do bees eat lunch?
Rad: At the bee-stro.

Dan: Why are you dancing with that jar?
Fran: It says, "To open, twist."

Q: What's a polar bear's favorite writing utensil?
A: A ballpoint penguin.

Q: What wise bird hangs out in the bathroom?
A: A hoo-towel.

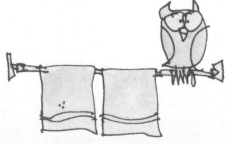

Q: Where do fish get clean?

A: In their bass tub.

Roommate #1: What's the best way to keep your hair dry in the shower?

Roommate #2: Don't turn on the water.

Susannah: What do you call someone who sees a crime in the rain?

Rose: An eye-wetness.

Q: What do you call a dog who's really dirty and needs a bath?

A: A germy shepherd.

Len: Why did the policeman always carry a
bar of soap with him?

Ben: Because he worked in a city with a high
grime rate.

Q: What do you call a six-pack of ducks?

A: A box of quackers.

Q: What's a bumblebee's favorite music?

A: Bee-bop.

Q: What kind of opera star sings in the shower?

A: A soap-rano.

Q: How can you tell when you're in a snake family's bathroom?

A: The towels say *Hiss* and *Hers*.

Rose: Why are you standing in front of the mirror with your eyes closed?

Rowan: I want to see what I look like when I'm asleep.

Teacher: Max, use the word *diploma* in a sentence.

Max: When da sink's stopped up, we call diploma.

Harper: I'd like to donate my aquarium to the army.

Asher: Why would they want that?

Harper: I heard they needed more tanks.

Tongue Twisters

If Stu chews shoes, should Stu choose the shoes he chews?

Pirates' private property.

Three short sword sheaths.

On a lazy laser razor lies a laser ray eraser.

Phil: Why did the plumber quit work early yesterday?

Bill: He was drained.

Peg: I stopped dating the chiropractor.

Meg: Why was that?

Peg: I got tired of all his back talk.

Q: What did the pirate get on his math test?

A: Sea plus.

Q: What do you get when you cross a pig with an evergreen tree?

A: A porky-pine.

Q: How does a lifeguard get to work?

A: He carpools.

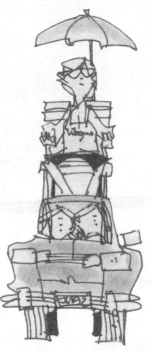

Q: What does the germ wear when he gets up in the morning?

A: His little microbe.

Iris: Why are you wearing that Zorro cape to bed?

Bo: I'm trying to catch some Zs.

Sweet dreams!

Jess: What does a chimney sweep carry with him at all times?

Fess: His soot-case.

Harper: Why did you invite that baseball player to go camping with us?

Asher: I needed someone to pitch the tent.

Remy: Why is Sir Lancelot always so tired?

Isabel: 'Cause he works the knight shift.

I turned vegan, but I think it's a big missed steak.

Did you hear about the little old woman who lived in a sock? Her shoe was being soled.

Q: What do bakers read to their kids at night?

A: Bread-time stories.

Q: What do you get when you cross a dentist with a boat?

A: A tooth ferry.

Q: Where does Santa stay when he's on vacation?

A: At a ho, ho, hotel.

Q: What's a cow's favorite night?

A: One with a full mooooon.

Braeden: What can dunk, knows how to dribble, and is three and a half feet tall?

Caden: A seven-foot basketball player taking a bow.

Q: What do you get when you cross a sheep with a monkey?

A: A baa-boon.

Mike: What do you get when you cross an elephant with a kangaroo?

Ike: Great big holes all over the jungle.

Q: Where do giraffes go to learn?

A: High school.

Dog: Hey, Cow, what are you doing?
Cow: Shhh, I'm on a steak-out.

When fish are in schools, they sometimes take debate.

Connor: Did you hear about the dry cleaner who was always late?
Chloe: Yeah, he was pressed for time.

Man: Sorry I'm late; I just got here. I'm sick.
Doctor: Flu?
Man: No, I took a bus.

Mom: Don't you ever let me catch you doing that again!
Kid: I'll try, but you're so quiet sometimes.

Q: **What do you get when you cross Christmas with St. Patrick's Day?**

A: St. O'Claus.

Bill: Why are you wearing that wet suit?
Jill: I'm going to a wedding shower.

Q: What's a duck's favorite part of the Constitution?

A: The Bill of Rights.

Q: What did the lumberjack do after he cut down the tree?

A: He took a bough.

Backward Jokes

Backward jokes give the answer first, then the question. Here's an example:

Answer: UCLA.

Question: What happens when the smog clears in Southern California?

Get the idea? So, go ahead and check these out:

Answer: 7 Up.

Question: What happens at Snow White's house
when the alarm clock goes off?

Okay, everybody, time to get up!

Answer: Dr Pepper.

Question: Who married Nurse Salt?

Answer: In a class by himself.

Question: How do you describe an only child who's homeschooled?

Answer: Descent.

Question: What's the difference between a cat and a skunk?

Answer: Doe-si-doe.

Question: What do you call two deer at a square dance?

Answer: Mississippi.

Question: What do you call a hippie's wife?

Answer: Satellite.

Question: What does the cowboy use to see after
dark?

Answer: Ranch dressing.

Question: What do you call it when you wear
cowboy clothes?

Answer: Laughingstock.

Question: What do you call cows with a good sense
of humor?

Answer: Modem.

Question: What did the landscaper do to the
lawns?

Answer: Analog.

Question: What does Ana throw into the fire?

Lonny: I don't trust stairs.
Donny: Why not?
Lonny: They're always up to something.

Ed: Which dogs bark more, young or old?
Ned: It's about arf and arf.

Q: How did pioneer puppies get out West?

A: They traveled in waggin' trains.

Q: What do you get when you cross a turtle with a boomerang?

A: Snappy comebacks.

Q: How did the cows get away from Farmer Brown's farm?

A: They used a mooooving van.

Q: How did the lambs get to the moon?

A: By space-sheep.

Why do people say "tuna fish" when they don't say "beef mammal" or "chicken bird"?

Q: What does a snake give its babies before bed?

A: Hugs and hisses.

Donny: What do you call a bunch of little dogs with cameras?

Lonny: Pup-arazzi.

Q: What do you get when you cross a pouting child with a rhino?

A: A whine-oceros.

I'm hungry, when do we eat?
Why's it so hot in here? Turn on the
air conditioning! Why do we have to
wait so long?

Deagan: Why are you ironing that four-leaf clover?

Hannah: I'm trying to press my luck.

Q: **Who leaps over tall buildings in order to wake people up?**

A: Clock Kent.

Q: **What do you call a flock of sheep rolling down a hill?**

A: A lamb-slide.

Brian: Why do pirates have such a hard time learning the alphabet?

Ryan: Because they sometimes get stuck at C for years. And then they get caught at *AAAARRRRRR.*

Knock, knock.
Who's there?

Baby owl.
Baby owl who?

Baby owl see you when you open the door.

Knock, knock.
Who's there?

Alpaca.
Alpaca who?

Alpaca trunk, you pack a suitcase, then we'll go on vacation.

Knock, knock.
Who's there?

Colleen.
Colleen who?

Colleen up this mess out here.

Q: What do you get when you cross a chicken with a skunk?

A: A fowl smell.

Have you heard the rumor about the peanut butter? I'd better not tell you; it might spread.

Q: Why couldn't the lamb get up in time?

A: He was still a sheep.

Q: What happens when you cross a painter with a police officer?

A: You have a brush with the law.

Q: Why did the boy study in the hot air balloon?

A: He wanted to get a higher education.

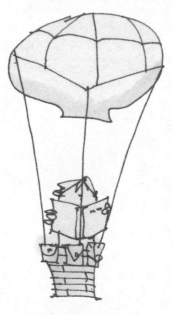

Q: What do you call a group of singing dinosaurs?

A: A tyranno-chorus.

Q: What do snowmen do on the weekend?

A: They chill out.

So, I was washing my car with my friend when he asked, "Why can't you just use a sponge?"

Q: Why did the boy sprinkle sugar on his pillow?

A: He wanted to have sweet dreams.

Q: What did one nut say to the nut he was chasing?

A: "I'm gonna cashew!"

Q: Why did the watchmaker enjoy his vacation so much?

A: He finally learned to unwind.

Jay: What does the Dentist of the Year receive?

Ray: A little plaque.

Q: Who is Santa's favorite singer?

A: Elfis Presley.

Ron: What do dentists call their dental X-rays?
John: Tooth pics.

SMILE!

Q: What city can never stay put?

A: Rome.

Q: What do you call a lazy kangaroo?

A: A pouch potato.

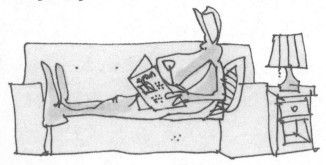

Q: What do you call a cinnamon bun who's at the top of the class?

A: An honor roll.

     Iris: Did you see the angry pancake?
     Bo: Yeah, he's ready to flip.

To be Frank, I'd have to change my name.

Joe: How does the shark from *Jaws* like his
breakfast eggs?
Flo: Terri-fried!

Q: How do leaves travel around?

A: By autumn-mobile.

I have a fear of speed bumps, but I'm slowly getting
over it.

Ava: Did you hear about the frog that got a job at a hotel?

Susannah: Really? What job?

Ava: He's a bellhop.

I need you to take these to room 407 and hop to it!

Q: What plants do chickens grow on?

A: Eggplants.

Peg: What colors would you paint the sun and the wind?

Meg: I'd paint the sun rose and the wind blue.

Knock, knock.
Who's there?

Juno.
Juno who?

Juno I'm out here, right?

Knock, knock.
Who's there?

Yacht.
Yacht who?

Yacht to know by now.

Tongue Twisters

Two tiny tigers took two taxis to town.

Dust is a disk's worst enemy.

She sees cheese.

Crush grapes, grapes crush, crush grapes.

Q: What's the richest kind of air?
 A: Billionaire.

If you have any good fish puns, let minnow.

Q: What do you call a rabbit who's really cool?
 A: A hip-hopper.

Q: What kind of driver never uses a car?
 A: A screwdriver.

Q: **What do you call a dinosaur who's always on time?**

A: A pronto-saurus.

Sorry I'm late.

Jim: What did the carpet say to the floor?
Tim: "Don't worry, I got you covered."

Knock, knock.
Who's there?
Albie.
Albie who?
Albie out here if you need me.

Q: How do cats decorate their houses?

A: With fur-niture.

Teacher: Sandy, name six wild animals.

Sandy: Two lions and four tigers.

Teacher: Are you chewing gum?

Jamie: No, ma'am, I'm Jamie Thompson.

Principal: Jackson, what time do you wake up in the morning?

Jackson: About an hour and a half after I get to school.

I just wrote a book on reverse psychology. Do *not* read it.

The other day my wife asked me to pass her the lipstick, and I accidentally passed her a glue stick instead. She still isn't talking to me.

Q: What sound does a chicken's phone make?

A: *Wing, wing.*

Q: What kind of dog lives at the North Pole?

A: A chili dog.

Q: What do you call a group of friends making a sweater?

A: Social knit-working.

Q: What's a little bear's favorite side dish?

A: Corn on the cub.

Mason: Did you hear about the dog who chased a stick for five miles?

Jason: That's pretty far-fetched.

Teacher: Why are you crawling into my classroom?

Max: Because you said, "Don't anyone dare walk in late!"

Teacher: Maddie, you copied Christy's paper, didn't you?

Maddie: How did you know?

Teacher: Well, for one, an answer on Christy's paper says, "I don't know," and yours says, "Me neither."

Dad: Matthew, this says you're at the bottom of your class of twenty. That's terrible!

Matthew: It could be worse.

Dad: How?

Matthew: It could have been a bigger class.

Jon: What are you doing, Ron?

Ron: Writing a letter to myself.

Jon: What does it say?

Ron: I don't know; I won't get it till tomorrow.

Teacher: Jon, how many *i*'s do you use to spell *Mississippi*?

Jon: None. I can do it blindfolded.

Teacher: What's your name, young man?

Kid: Henry.

Teacher: Excuse me, you need to say *sir*!

Kid: Okay. Sir Henry.

I love elevator jokes. They work on so many levels.

Teacher: I'm happy to give you a 70 in science.

Bo: Why don't you really enjoy yourself and give me a 100?

Asher: I can't go to school today; I don't feel well.

Mom: Where don't you feel well?

Asher: In school.

The brain is an amazing instrument. It starts working the minute you wake up in the morning, and it never stops until you're called on in class.

Diner: Waiter, what is this fly doing in my soup?

Waiter: Looks like the Macarena.

Kylie makes a phone call to her aunt's house.

Kylie: Hi, may I speak to Jonah please?

Aunt: Why, Jonah's only a baby. He hasn't learned to talk yet.

Kylie: That's okay. I'll hold.

Little Girl: How much are these diapers?

Clerk: Nine dollars plus tax.

Little Girl: Oh, that's okay. We don't need the tacks; my mom uses safety pins.

Al: Is your sister spoiled?

Sal: No, that's just the perfume she wears.

These shoes will be tight for the next two weeks.

Okay, I'll start wearing them the third week.

A woman was walking down the street one afternoon when she saw a small boy trying to reach the doorbell of a nearby house. Sensing his frustration, she walked up on the porch and pushed the doorbell for him. Then she turned to him and said, "What do we do now, young man?"

"Run!" he said, and he took off.

Charlotte: How did the mice do in school?
Susannah: They just squeaked by.

Lawyer: Why is the judge sending for the
          locksmith?
Bailiff: Oh, the key witness is missing.

Q: What's 5,700 feet tall and has four heads?

A: Mount Rushmore.

Q: What's a frog's favorite musical instrument?

A: A hop-sichord.

A clown held the door open for me this morning. I
thought it was a nice jester.

I asked the lion in my wardrobe what he was doing there. He said, "Narnia business."

Q: Why did the pie go to the dentist?

A: To get a filling.

Q: What kind of bird works at a construction site?

A: A crane.

Q: What do you call an alligator who's a thief?

A: A crookodile.

Q: Why did the tree surgeon open another office?

A: He was branching out.

Couldn't figure out how to work my seat belt. Then it clicked.

Judge: The charge is stealing a blanket. How do you plead?

Defendant: Not quilty.

Q: What's Santa's favorite sandwich?

A: Peanut butter and jolly.

Q: Where do penguins keep their money?

A: In snowbanks.

Talk about cold cash.

Terry: Why was the swim instructor fired?
Jerry: He kept people wading too long.

Q: What is gray, weighs three tons, and soars through the air?

A: A hippo on a hang glider.

Q: What did the skeleton order at the restaurant?

A: Spare ribs.

Customer: May I have a pair of alligator shoes, please?

Shoe Salesperson: Certainly. What size is your alligator?

Q: Where do you go to weigh a whale?

A: To the whale-weigh station.

Teacher: Max, describe a synonym.

Max: It's a word you use when you can't spell the other word.

Teacher: Tyler, what comes before March?
Tyler: Forward!

Teacher: Did your father help you on this assignment?
Caden: Nope, he did it all on his own.

Man: I've been riding this bus to work for fifteen years now.
Lady: Oh my goodness, where did you get on?

Donny: The trombone player lost his job in the band.

Lonny: Why?

Donny: He just kept letting things slide.

A little boy swallowed a quarter and two dimes. When his mom took him to the doctor, they took an X-ray.

"I think he's going to be fine," the doctor said as he looked at the picture.

"Why do you say that?" the mom asked.

"I don't see any change in him," the doctor answered.

Reporter: Congratulations! You actually cloned yourself! How do you feel?

Scientist: I'm beside myself!

Teacher: Harper, use the word *folder* in a sentence.
Harper: We need to show respect folder people.

A deer, a skunk, and a duck were at a diner. When the check came, the deer had no doe and the skunk didn't have a scent, so the duck said, "Put it on my bill."

Al: I don't have a cent to my name.
Sal: Are you going to get a job?
Al: No, I'm gonna change my name.

Max: I put five dollars in the change machine.
Alsea: What happened?
Max: Would you believe it? I'm still me.

Mrs. Taylor: Doctor, my husband is convinced he's a
                     boomerang.
   Doctor: Don't worry, he'll come around.

Tongue Twisters

Busy buzzing bumblebees.

No need to light a night-light on a light night like
   tonight.

Many an anemone sees an enemy anemone.

Lesser leather never weathered wetter weather better.

I've made my lawn chicken-proof. Now it's impeccable.

Dan: Rats! I left my watch back there on top of the hill.

Jan: Should you go get it?

Dan: No, it'll run down by itself.

Ryan: Everyone says I got my good looks from my father.

Brian: Oh, is he a plastic surgeon?

Mom: Liam, there were two cookies in the jar last night, and now there is only one. Can you explain that?

Liam: Yeah, it was so dark I missed it.

Jon: Mom, I won the election for class president!

Mom: Honestly?

Jon: Did you have to bring that up?

Q: What do you get when you cross a chicken with a robber?

A: A peck-pocket.

Q: What's long and orange and flies at the speed of sound?

A: A jet-propelled carrot.

Teacher: If you received ten dollars from ten people, what would you get?

Jamie: A new bike!

Teacher: What birds do you find in Portugal?
     Kid: Portu-geese!

Principal: Do you know a kid named Alex?
       Kid: Yup, he sleeps right next to me in geometry.

Teacher: What do you call the little rivers that feed into the Nile?
     Kid: Juvi-Niles!

Knock, knock.
Who's there?

Aubrey.
Aubrey who?

Aubrey quiet!

Why are you staring at that can
of frozen orange juice?

The label says, "Concentrate."

Knock, knock.
Who's there?

Ivan.
Ivan who?

Ivan idea you know who this is.

    Stan: Is this a good lake for fish?

    Dan: It must be; I can't get any of them to come out.

A lady is sitting on the train as it creeps through the countryside. Finally, she finds the conductor.

    Lady: This is the slowest train I've ever been on. Can't you run any faster?

Conductor: Sure, but they make me stay on the train.

Emily Biddle Returns

Librarian Emily Biddle has a collection of unusual books in her bookmobile.

Book Titles:

Building an Igloo **by S. K. Moe**
Keep Things Oiled **by Russ T. Gates**
I Hate the Daytime **by Gladys Knight**
I Didn't Do It! **by Ivan Alibi**
A Spring Shower **by Wayne Dwops**
Tiny Fish **by Ann Chovie**
Stop Arguing **by Xavier Breath**
Off to Market **by Tobias A. Pig**
The New Floor **by Lynn O'Leum**
House Construction **by Bill Jerome Holme**

More Book Titles:

Discover Chicago **by D. Wendy City**
You've Got to Be Kidding! **by Shirley U. Jest**
Why Wait? Let's Go! **by Igor Beaver**
Keep Your House Clean **by Lotta Dust**
Come on In! **by Doris Open**
Winning the Race **by Vic Tree**
Hot Dog! **by Frank Furter**
Exploring the Backwoods **by Dusty Rhoads**
Dress Like the 70s **by Polly Esther**
Learn Fractions **by Lois Denominator**

Sandy Silverthorne, author of *Crack Yourself Up Jokes for Kids* and *More Crack Yourself Up Jokes for Kids*, has been writing and illustrating books since 1988 and currently has over 600,000 copies in print. His award-winning Great Bible Adventure children's series with Harvest House sold over 170,000 copies and has been distributed in eight languages worldwide. He has written and illustrated over thirty books and has worked with such diverse clients as Universal Studios Tour, Doubleday Publishers, Penguin, World Vision, the University of Oregon, the Charlotte Hornets, and the Academy of Television Arts and Sciences. His One-Minute Mysteries series has sold over 240,000 copies. Sandy has worked as a cartoonist, author, illustrator, actor, pastor, speaker, and comedian. Apparently, it's hard for him to focus. Connect with him at sandysilverthornebooks.com.